Thought Leaders Aren't Robots:

*7 Strategies and 10 Tactics
to Become a Thought Leader*

F. Annie Pettit, PhD, FCRIC

Second Printing: 2024
ISBN-13: 978-1540644923

Be yourself.

Table of Contents

Introduction

You can't grab a name tag, scribble the word 'Thought Leader" on it, and be a Thought Leader. It's no different for a company. You can't bestow upon your company a creative tagline like 'Thought Leaders in Our Industry' and be a Thought Leader.

That's not how it works. (Cue oblivious Michael Scott from The Office TV show hollering "I DECLARE BANKRUPTCY" at his stunned colleagues.)

Becoming a Thought Leader doesn't happen overnight and, in many cases, it happens without intent or planning. It requires a state of mind and way of being, combined with a clear process that takes time and commitment. Becoming a Thought Leader, though, is worthwhile for you and for the people around you.

Being a Thought Leader means that people have learned to seek out your advice and opinions because you have proven your insights are unique and meaningful, your expertise is trustworthy, you seek to remain at the forefront of knowledge in your field, you are open to being respectfully challenged on your opinions. and you are genuinely happy to share that knowledge with people.

Other than being personally fulfilling, being a Thought Leader brings advantages and opportunities. For instance:

- Your increased knowledge of your industry will allow you to do your job with greater perspective and relevance
- You will always know who to turn to when you need expert advice

- You will get to know people around the world, from countries and continents you have never visited, many of whom you would have never otherwise met nor heard of
- You will have more chances to meet and bask in the glow of some of your industry heroes
- Your heroes might ask you to write an article or book with them, or even speak at a conference with them
- Industry associations may ask for your expertise in the development of standards, guidelines, and for your participation in other important industry discussions
- Potential clients may seek out your expertise such that you spend less time hunting for new business
- You may never be truly unemployed since new opportunities will be regularly offered to you
- You will always have lots of people to hang out, chat, tour, and eat with at conferences and events
- You might be paid to ~~go on holidays~~ travel to and speak at meetings and conferences around the world

Of course, being a Thought Leader also has disadvantages.

- You will lose some of your anonymity
- You will have to think twice before publicly saying the ridiculous things you used to say so freely
- You might have less free time since more people will seek out your advice
- You will have to learn to say no because it is impossible to help every person who is keen to learn (although writing a book like this is a great way to share your knowledge with many people)

Overall, being a Thought Leader is a good thing, and in our own way, each of us should strive to be one. It's good for our personal growth and it's good for business. And if you do arrive at the ultimate destination, it's a humbling experience.

Whether becoming a Thought Leader is a personal goal for you or a company goal for your entire team, I hope the seven strategies and ten tactics outlined in this book guide you well in your quest. Good luck!

How to be a Thought Leader

7 Strategies

1. Recognize your expertise

I have a habit of nudging people I've just met to speak at conferences or write blog posts with me. In many cases, they decline because they aren't an expert in anything. Or so they believe.

The idea that you are not an expert is false.

Every one of us is an expert in something. You just need to figure out what your expertise is.

Think about what you learned during your post-secondary education, your apprenticeship, college, or university experience. You specialized in a field that almost no one else in the world knows anything about. Less than half of people have college degrees, and only a tiny percentage of those people pursued and successfully completed the specialization that you chose. Your knowledge is rare even if you work with ten other people who also earned that designation.

Think about the classes, seminars, and workshops you've completed. You learned extremely specialized skills and techniques in those classes, and you learned from someone who taught those skills based on their unique life experiences. No one else interpreted that training in the same way that you did.

Think about what you've learned at your jobs. The set of tasks, projects, clients, colleagues, managers, companies, successes, problems, and mistakes you've experienced are unique to you. The ten people sitting beside you, the ones with the same designations, did not experience nor learn from them in the same way you did. Your experiences and interpretations of those experiences are unique.

Think about what you learned growing up. Rich or poor, black or white, Jewish or Muslim, city boy or country girl, jock or nerd, shy or outgoing, you collected and learned from a unique set of experiences presented to you by your friends, family, neighbours, teachers, culture, city, and country.

You are unique. Your expertise is unique.

Stop thinking that the word Expert refers to the sole individual on planet Earth who knows everything about a certain thing. The world cannot function with one expert in their own silo. People thrive by learning from many experts with diverging and contradictory opinions, and you are one of those experts.

Part of the problem is that terrible thing called Imposter Syndrome, something that occurs when you think that other people are smarter, better, and more informed, and that you aren't worthy or comparable to them. Well, maybe other people are smarter or more experienced. To be honest, I don't care. Let them be smarter, better, and more informed. It doesn't mean that you are *not* smart, *not* great, and *not* informed. And it certainly doesn't mean that you aren't worthy. That's a whole lot of inaccurate BS coming from your misinformed brain.

Let's take an example of a 'lowly' project manager who does the same set of highly prescriptive and non-negotiable tasks every day. How could this person be an expert in anything of importance? In oh so many ways.

This lowly project manager could teach people:

- *The ten mistakes continually encountered in this type of role and how these mistakes can be prevented.*

- *What types of projects are more likely to be successful and how to ensure your project has these features.*

- *How to fine-tune the entire process so that tasks are completed more efficiently and with fewer errors.*

- *How to communicate with different people in different ways, and convince each person to complete their part of the work more accurately and quickly.*

- *How to identify and manage risks throughout the project life cycle*

- *How to best manage budgeting and costs to stay within constraints*

This lowly project manager needs to notice how not lowly they are, but rather how much of an expert they truly are in their daily tasks. There is an expert in there, in everyone. It just might take time and effort to recognize what those areas of expertise are.

Look inward

If you're struggling to figure out what your expertise is, one thing you can try is keeping a journal to track your skills, accomplishments, and the challenges you've faced. It doesn't need to be detailed or emotional. Simply note things like:

- *New software you learned*

- *A new feature or function you learned within the software*

- *A problem you encountered with a colleague or client, and the tactics you took to resolve it*

- *The task you most enjoyed doing that day*

- *Complements received from your manager, colleagues, or clients*
- *What advice do colleague seek from you*
- *Things you admire about your colleagues*
- *Training, workshops, or conferences you'd love to attend, r things you loved about the session you just attended*

Over time, that collection of notes will become an objective description of who you are and how you shine.

Get insights from others

In addition to looking inwards, ask other people. Your colleagues, manager, clients, mentors, and partner will all have different experiences with and perceptions of you. They aren't wearing the huge set of blinders you are so their feedback may offer a unique and unbiased view of your expertise that you hadn't considered.

Get insights from job search websites

Alternatively, head over a job search website and review the skills that managers advertise for. Don't even worry about narrowing down the jobs to those that are similar to yours. Many of the most important skills are broadly relevant and generalize across occupations. If you can be honest with yourself, you'll find at least a few skills like these that accurately reflect you.

- *Active listening*
- *Adaptability*
- *Attention to detail*
- *Creativity*
- *Critical thinking*
- *Customer service*
- *Ethics*
- *Interpersonal skills*
- *Leadership*
- *Management*
- *Marketing*
- *Organization*

- *Data analysis*
- *Decision making*
- *Design*
- *Empathy*
- *Presentation*
- *Problem solving*
- *Teamwork*
- *Written communication*

You're not an expert in everything.

Once you've identified what you *are* an expert in, take the time to accept that you're *not* an expert in other things. Being an expert in one area of your industry does not mean you're an expert in every area, even if you took a class or workshop on it.

Thought Leaders feel no shame in admitting what they don't know. Indeed, Thought Leaders are quick to point out when they are not the expert because it means they can steer you towards several trustworthy people who *are* experts.

Thought Leaders have a broad understanding of their industry which includes knowing other key experts in that industry. If you can't be the expert, you can be an expert in knowing who is the expert.

2. Focus on your expertise

Now that you have an idea of what your expertise is, you need to focus on that area and create balance in the content you put out for public consumption, whether verbal or in writing. The hundreds of Facebook, Instagram, and TikTok posts you love to share about all of your cooking adventures will not advance your long-term goal unless you plan to be a foodie Thought Leader. Balancing a few irrelevant status updates is important and desirable, but most of your content should relate to your primary focus.

Identify your primary focus

First, you need to clarity your general or primary focus. For most people, it's reasonably easy to identify the industry or department you work in (or want to work in). It's probably something like human resources, education, engineering, medicine, art, construction, hospitality, cooking, health, or some other broad category.

Going forward, in everything you do, leverage your general focus to demonstrate your understanding of current industry issues, and how they are relevant to your business and potential clients. Your content should demonstrate that you:

- *Know the strengths and weaknesses in your industry*
- *Understand the pros and cons of current techniques and processes*
- *Are aware of the hot buttons and fads that everyone is talking about.*
- *Can understand and respond to both sides of controversial issues*
- *Can generate creative and innovative ideas of your own*

- *Are forward thinking about where your industry is headed*
- *Seek out and learn new ideas*

Whether you're writing blog posts and articles, or speaking on podcasts and at events, you need to demonstrate your breadth of knowledge and your ability to offer intelligent guidance in broad, relevant areas. The goal isn't to demonstrate expertise in all areas, but rather to demonstrate general intelligence and insight about your place in the industry.

Identify your secondary focus

Second, clarify your area of expertise. This requires that you actively consider whether you plan to continue in your current area of expertise, or shift in the short-term or long-term to a different direction. You can't be all things to all people so choose a secondary focus that best suits you and your future.

For example, a market researcher might have a specific focus in quantitative market research methods like questionnaire design, research design, research panels, and analytics. However, in the future, they might want to pivot to broader interests like neuroscience and biometrics. Given these areas of focus, this market researcher might focus their content very generally on a wide range of things related to market research but then get specific and technical when conversations turn to questionnaire techniques and research design.

The following table gives a few examples how different experts might lay out what will be their primary and secondary expert focus areas.

General focus	Expert focus options
Market Research	Questionnaire design
	Biometrics
	Neuroscience
	Focus groups
	Analytics
	Education
Marketing	Influencer marketing
	Affiliate marketing
	Optimization
	Social media
	Omni-channel
	Innovation
Human Resources	Recruiting and staffing
	Benefits design and admin
	Training
	Employee relations
	Employee engagement
	Diversity, equity, and inclusion
Education	Special education
	STEM education
	Adult education
	Online learning
	International education
Journalism	Data journalism
	Sport journalism
	Technical writing
	Copy writing
	Photojournalism

Once you identify your general and expert areas of focus, take time two or three times each year to evaluate everything you put out into your space and determine how well your plan matches reality.

- *Do you focus too much on personal or off-topic issues such that you're becoming known for your origami skills rather than your journalism skills?*

- *Have your talks and posts branched off into a different secondary focus because you discovered a hip new fad?*

- *Do you need to get back on track or do you need to adjust your primary or secondary focus onto a new path?*

- *Have you drifted away from your general focus such that potential clients only remember you when they need to actively search out experts in your field?*

Thought Leaders know how to focus.

3. Be genuine

If you already use a social network tool like LinkedIn, Facebook, Instagram, or TikTok, peek at it right now and see if your most recent 50 posts look something like this.

Check out our new products here
Please register for our webinar here
Schedule a meeting to learn about our products
Thank you for following us
Tell us what you think about our products
Thank you for the share
Thank you for your comment
Please download our white paper

These messages do not demonstrate Thought Leadership. In fact, they demonstrate no thought. They don't highlight innovation and insight. They don't build meaningful and long-lasting relationships. Rather, these types of messages build character counts, status counts, and fake follower counts. They're sales devices and they're boring. These kinds of messages will make people in your target audience stop following you.

People inherently want relationships with other people. Think about the people you most look forward to chatting with, your friends and your family. Why do you look forward to chatting them in particular? Because they listen to you, they're interesting, and they have personality.

They laugh and joke and say weird things. They go off-topic, share silly stories, and do ridiculous things. They care about you, and they're interested in how you feel and what you're doing. This is how to people. Given that you're a people too, potentially a Thought Leader people, you need to carry that style of your personal life into your business life.

Being fun and genuine doesn't mean you need to create a content plan that includes one cartoon every Monday at 1pm, one comic every Wednesday at 10am, and one joke every Friday at 4pm.

Instead, a human personality must shine through in everything you do. If a large majority of your activities relate to your general focus and your area of expertise, then a minority of your content must show people that you are a genuine human being who has outside interests as well.

Talk about how you messed up dinner, are excited to go to the game with your kids this weekend, or learned that horrid E major chord on the ukulele. And share that silly comic or joke that will make people in your industry groan with understanding. Whether it's your personal account or your company's business account, the humanness of the person running that account must come through.

At the same time, being genuine and human doesn't mean you must talk about your personal and private life, especially if the people involved haven't given consent. In fact, talking about your vacation plans or your home could create privacy and safety issues. If you must talk about your holidays, wait until after the fact so that people don't know when your giant TV is unattended.

Similarly, when it comes to your home, no one needs to see pictures of or hear you complain about renovations to your huge house or your second 'cottage' by the lake. Being genuine and respectful means you help people feel empowered, not inadequate and deprived.

6

Being genuine and human means that it's perfectly ok and recommended for Thought Leaders to communicate in a personal way, use casual language, share non-business content, and use words like 'I.'

Thanks a bunch for sharing that link
I love watching you present!
Your puppy is the cutest ever!
That donut looks delish! Fax me some!
Your new book looks just excellent! Congratulations!
I'm so happy you were promoted. Great job!
Your webinar was one of the best I've seen.
I loved how quirky you were on stage!
That's the best description of that technique I've seen.

Marketing campaigns go viral because they touch our hearts in some way. Babies, ponies, and quirky weirdness connect with us on a personal level. Did you ever see an advertisement with perfectly proportioned logos and precise lists of caveats and exceptions go viral? No.

Thought Leaders flourish because people connect with human beings, not logos and taglines.

4. Use your voice for good

When you become a Thought Leader, people will pounce on your words. Your posts and talks will get shared on a much wider scale and your opinions will reach people around the world in seconds. You need to think about how you offer and frame your content so that it creates good.

Be positive

Be conscious of how positive or negative your content is. People who constantly criticize other people's work are no fun to listen to nor learn from, no matter how 'right' they are.

As a long-term strategy, being overly critical is detrimental for you, your business, and your community. Thought Leaders should be critical but it needs to be done in a positive, respectful, and helpful way. I'm not a quote person but this is one of my favourites.

> *Great minds discuss ideas; average minds discuss events; small minds discuss people. [Originated with Henry Thomas Buckle, made famous by Eleanor Roosevelt]*

When criticism is necessary, criticize the processes, techniques, or interpretations and not the people behind them. And, consider whether a criticism can be made without context. Sometimes, generic examples or anonymized examples are better.

Further, consider whether a negative or critical commentary can be made positive without losing the thrust of the argument. For example, you might write a post or prepare a talk with titles like these:

> *Why I hate random samples*

Here's why clients hate you
This is why you're failing
The ugly reality behind influencer marketing
Why omni-channel is a waste of money
Avoid these 7 career-killing habits

If you almost never post negative content, then run with it. You don't need to be positive all the time. However, if you find that much of your recent content has fallen on the negative side, consider reframing your upcoming into a more positive informative post like these:

Ten ways to create a better random sample
Ten ways to make clients love you
5 innovative ways to be successful
How to succeed at influencer marketing
8 great tips to leverage omni-channel
Learn these 7 career-building habits

Support others

Using your voice for good also includes pulling people up the ladder with you. Regardless of how big or small your platform is, use it to help others.

- *Encourage people who need a little push, even when they work for your fiercest rival.*
- *When you learn someone won an award, congratulate them and share the news.*
- *When you see someone get their dream job, tell them how proud you are of them.*
- *Encourage great writers to write for their industry association blog.*

Become known as the person who is always ready to support others. Someone who helps others reach their personal goals and become better people.

Using your voice for good means figuring out what you stand for in life, outside of your brand and your company, and then supporting those causes.

Even before their voice is big, Thought Leaders use it to make the world a better place.

5. Be clickbait

Why do some educational and informative writers and speakers fail to become popular? Because they're boring. They lack personality. Anyone else in the industry could have said the same thing. They don't say anything new or different.

They don't use clickbait.

Typical social media clickbait relies on extravagant claims and ridiculous statements like these:

> *See how one man made $$$ answering questionnaires*
> *Invoicing departments HATE this new trick*
> *You Won't Believe the Secret Stock Tip That Made Investors Millions Overnight!*
> *Unveiling the Top 10 Tech Gadgets That Will Change Your Life Forever!*
> *Shocking Legal Loophole Exposed – How to Beat Any Court Case and Win Big!*
> *The Truth Behind the Headlines – Journalists Reveal the Stories You Weren't Meant to Know!*

Obviously, extravagant claims or ridiculous statements like these are not appropriate unless you work at The Onion. However, on your road to becoming a genuine, sought-after Thought Leader, when you encounter a new idea, new method, new process, new anything, think carefully about it and work through the range of opinions from logical to fanatical to nonsensical and ridiculous.

Listen to people from all around the world and read what they write. Find and consume as many disparate ideas and opinions as you can. When you've consumed all that knowledge, identify your own personal, unique opinion. And then...

Have an opinion.

Take the time to figure out what your opinion is. Listen to your brain. You have opinions on lots of things if you'd take the time to figure them out.

Once you've figured out what your opinion is, take an official stand. If you're balancing on the middle, jump to one side or the other. Don't have a neutral opinion. Don't waffle, and don't hover somewhere between liking and not liking. Take a stand and be For or Against, Pro or Con, Like or Dislike.

Amplify your stand.

Then, amp up your opinion so that you hinge on being almost uncomfortable with it. Do you think a new technique is great, an 8 out of 10? Well, now it's amazing, a 9 out of 10. Do you think that new process is really bad, a 3 out of 10? Well, now it's horrid, a 2 out of 10. Don't lie about or misconstrue your genuine opinion but have the courage to put your entire body and soul into that opinion. Be open to having an opinion that threatens other people's opinions. Be prepared to have your opinion challenged and be prepared to defend it.

One of the wonderful aspects of being a Thought Leader is that you get to be a part of a discussion in which people challenge assumptions and push the boundaries. By publicly emboldening your opinion, your audience may start to rethink their own opinions, their own reasoning. They'll wonder how you see something they don't. It results in deeper discussions and richer conversations. Challenge is okay. It's good.

Make your opinion unique.

Once you've settled on your emboldened opinion, find a way to make it unique. Add an unusual insight based on your personal experiences, or some data that only you have access to. Explain the issue using a perspective that has never been considered before. Find a way to make the issue vastly easier to understand.

Thought Leaders don't simply repeat opinions or information they've heard from other speakers or read from other writers. They re-interpret data and theories, provide alternate opinions, and add new insights based on their own set of experiences.

Thought Leaders challenge the status quo.

6. Don't be a sales pitch

Thought Leaders cannot be sales people. At least not in the traditional sense.

People turn to Thought Leaders for their freely offered, trustworthy and unbiased opinions and insights, not only about products and services from their own company, but from other companies as well.

Thought Leaders can discuss pros and cons without being unfairly biased in favour of their own company. Yes, they can promote their own products and services, but only once they truly believe those are the most suitable options for a very specific case. If you can't offer unbiased opinions, even about your own company, you won't be a Thought Leader.

People get more than enough sales pitches in every aspect of their lives. Every email, newsletter, social media status message, phone call, and conference presentation is a potential sales pitch. They don't need yet another sales pitch. What they do need is someone they can trust to give them a fair and unbiased opinion.

Falling into the sales pitch trap can happen in several ways so let's review the easiest traps.

Sales meetings

There is no reason a Thought Leader can't take part in a sales meeting. But, think carefully about the role you take. If you *are* the sales lead, then be the sales lead. If you are the content expert or Thought Leader, focus on that role. Don't simply talk about the good aspects of your company or your products. Be the wise person who listens carefully to the client's needs and then explains the good and the bad, how the products will and won't work, and what the better options might be. Be a product expert that potential clients trust because you always explain the important issues, not just the issues that will help you win the job.

Open calls for recommendations

It's easy to fall into sales discussions on the interweebs. People will post on their LinkedIn page (or whichever social media network that is most suitable for their industry) that they are outright seeking recommendations for products and services. If you're lucky, you'll know that your product is best suited for their needs.

However, if you want to be known as a Thought Leader, your first intention should always be to reply to those types of posts with insightful guidance that will help them with the entirety of their issue, not to sell them on your company as fast as you possibly can.

Listen and learn, then advise and recommend.

Blogging and speaking

Blogs and conference speeches are huge offenders of trying to simultaneously demonstrate Thought Leadership and sell their products. You'll regularly see or hear phrases like:

> *At Annie Pettit Consulting, we recommend using random samples whenever possible.*

> *We used our own panel, the proprietary Annie Pettit World Superior panel with globally recognized and unmatched data quality processes, to conduct this research on bar soap usage.*

No one wants to hear you say 'at our company' or spout the taglines of your proprietary techniques. No one thinks you're talking about a competitor's product on your own blog, particularly when the side bar, header, and footer all mention your products by name.

Get rid of the off-putting sales pitch phrasing, and choose personal and genuine phrasing instead:

> *I recommend using random samples whenever possible.*
>
> *We used our own opt-in panel to conduct this research on bar soap usage.*

Newsletters

Many people use emailed newsletters to help current clients and prospects learn more about them (and not forget them). One sure-fire way to make people stop reading those newsletters and eventually unsubscribe or block you is to use bait and switch tactics.

Don't collect email addresses with the promise of sharing conference photos and then add those people to your newsletter email list. Don't tell people you'd like to send them newsletters about industry hot buttons and then fill those newsletters with sales pitches. Don't bait and switch.

So what kind of selling *can* you do?

Well, if you think about everything a Thought Leader does, every bit of it is selling. It's the quiet logo in the corner of the PowerPoint presentation, and the bio at the end of the white paper. It's the transparency and trust a Thought Leader becomes known for that convinces clients to hire them. It's the unique insights and interpretations that can't be found anywhere else that attracts clients.

It's a different style of selling, a low key, non-threatening sell. It might take longer, but a well-written, informative, and educational blog post is far more effective at building your Thought Leadership status and long-term client relationships than an overt sales pitch.

Thought Leaders don't sell products. They sell trust.

7. Choose wisely

Every Thought Leader does things a bit differently. Some have never written a blog, some have never written a book, some have never recorded a podcast, but all of them use at least a few of the tactics described in this book.

You don't need to use every tactic, but you do need to figure out which ones suit your personal style. If you're an extravert, choose the face-to-face, speak, meet, and talk options. Use your out-going and chatty nature to your advantage.

If you're an introvert, have no fear. Many of the tactics described here can be done from your couch while wearing pajamas. You *can* build meaningful relationships and become an influential person without ever leaving your home.

The best way to start is slow.

Choose one tactic you can do well and succeed at quickly. If you're stuck on transit for an hour every day, use that time to write a 200 to 300 word, lightning fast blog post every week. Commit to writing one substantive comment on LinkedIn every week. Download TikTok and share one post from a relevant content creator every week.

When you finally decide on the tactics that are right for you, start doing them right away. Don't wait for your boss to encourage you, or a mentor to push you, or a colleague to recommend you. As the saying goes, the harder you work, the more good luck you will have. *Ask* for the things you want.

Regardless of how you start, the important part is that you start. Choose one thing and start.

Thought Leaders listen to Nike. They just do it.

Tactics

1. Leverage your credentials

Credentials come in many forms but none of them will help you if modesty prevents you from sharing them. Include them on your social media accounts, on your blog, in your email signature line, and in your speaker and author bios. There's no reason to constantly remind people about them but make sure the information is readily available should someone wish to find it.

Professoinal degrees

For many professionals, a Bachelor's degree is the price of entry. If you have relevant certificates/diplomas, or a Master's degree, Doctorate, or something similar, make sure they're obvious.

If you do have a Doctorate, you don't need to insist that people address you as Doctor. However, you do need to make sure that when the occasion demands it, any titles you have earned are used. Ensuring the appropriate use of your title is especially true for women who may occasionally find their titles are ignored. If you're in a situation where other people are addressed as 'Dr' and you're addressed as 'Ms,' make sure to speak up and request the same level of respect.

Industry certifications

If your industry association offers a certification program, consider applying for it particularly if your formal education is in an unrelated field. Many types of certification programs are available, from being SAS or CISCO Certified in the tech world, to being a Professional Project Manager. Make sure all of these certifications are visible somewhere on your personal website and your social media 'About me' pages.

Workshops

If you've completed workshops to enhance your personal or technical skills, these count too. It's important for people to know that you, as a Thought Leader, place value on self-development. That you're not above being the student rather than the teacher. Include that one day workshop on presentation skills, data visualization, writing skills, or working with difficult people on your professional LinkedIn page and your personal website. And continue to participating in self-directed learning.

Memberships

At a minimum, become a member of your industry's national association or society. Where finances allow, branch out to one or two other relevant associations to demonstrate your awareness and respect of global issues in your industry. Again, make sure this information is findable in your digital profiles.

Awards

Not everyone wins awards so make sure yours are front and center. Be sure your digital profiles highlights association awards, internal company awards, and community awards, all of which demonstrate your commitment to quality, expertise, education, and good will.

More importantly, don't wait for awards to fall in your lap. Take some time every year review association websites in your industry and identify any awards they may be offer. Figure out which ones you qualify for and nominate yourself for them. Enlist the help of a colleague or friend if necessary. And while you're at it, nominate colleagues who also deserve to win, even if they're from competing companies. Thought Leaders don't ignore other deserving people in order to better their own chances.

Affiliations

Be transparent about any long-term or significant volunteer work you do for industry and community associations. Not being paid for something doesn't mean it isn't important or meaningful. If you've been volunteering for ten years, it proves you care about things other than yourself.

If you don't already volunteer with an association, consider this your personal invitation. Find one right now and figure out how you can best help them.

2. Always be learning

Companies and their employees are often silos of information sharing. We share ideas with colleagues who share them with other colleagues who parrot them back to us. Since everyone uses the same Kool-Aid machine, innovation of thought can be difficult.

The only way to learn and stay up-to-date is to go places you don't usually go, read things you don't usually read, and listen to people you don't normally listen to. Seek out new ideas and differences of opinion. Challenge yourself and grow your mind. Resolve to take 15 to 30 minutes every day to listen and learn using whichever resource best suits you.

The internet is so very much our friend. There are unending places to learn but let's start with a few basic ones.

Microblogging social media platforms

Sites like Mastodon, Tumblr, and Twitter (or whatever we're calling it now) are a treasure trove of links to highly relevant industry news, white papers, webinars, rants and raves, conferences, news articles, and more.

If you're not already using one of these sties, here are some basic tips to get started using them effectively for Thought Leadership purposes.

- After registering yourself for an account, immediately follow as many people in your industry as the network allows. If it lets you follow 2000 people right away, then do so. If it only lets you follow 100 people per day, then follow 100 people each day for the next ten days. Following this many people might seem excessive or needy but what it really means is that your stream will always be populated with fresh, up-to-the-minute, industry relevant news.

- DO identify and follow the key people relevant to your primary and secondary focus areas. Further, look at who they are following and follow those people yourself.

- DO search out the local, national, and global associations in your industry and follow them. Look also for the secondary or peripheral associations. Make sure to also follow the associations in other countries where you can read the language.

- Do NOT follow celebrities unless they are ambassadors for your industry. (Or you genuinely like their opinions.)

- If you want to listen to non-industry people, consider adding them to a separate list or account rather than following them or including them in your main account. That way, you can choose your mood. For instance, I keep lists of Canadian researchers, women researchers, and academic comedians. When I'm in the mood for the sillies, I open the comedian list and chuckle away. When I'm in the mood to share content from fellow Canadians, I open that list instead.

- Do NOT follow someone just because they followed you. Perhaps it feels polite but you oversee your social media stream, not them. You decide who and what interests you.

- DO unfollow people if you realize you are no longer interested in their content. If you don't like someone's use of profanity, their inspirational quotes, or their posts about grain silos, it is your right to unfollow them.

- DO follow and message anyone, including famous people, world leaders, and industry icons. Many social media networks are public places where anyone is allowed and encouraged to communicate with everyone. There are no pedestals. At least, there should be no pedestals.

- Do NOT read or follow up on everything in your stream. Read a few messages when you feel like it. Ignore the messages that don't interest you. You are the boss of your stream, and you can open and close the site whenever you like.

LinkedIn for professionals

Compared to broad social media sites, LinkedIn is a professional site designed for career development, job searching, and professional networking. It takes much longer to grow a large network on LinkedIn but once you follow many people and companies, your stream will always have fresh articles, ideas, and comments to learn from. There are a few tactics to keep in mind.

- Connect with anyone in your industry, or anyone who touches your industry, regardless of whether you have met or talked to them. Every link is a knowledgeable person who might:
  Reveal amazing insights into your industry
  Identfiy other experts you should listen to
  Share industry news that is highly relevant for you
  Teach you something in one of their blog posts
  Offer interesting comments on your blog posts
  Write a guest post for your company blog
  Want to write an article for your magazine

> *Ask you write an article for their magazine*
> *Speak at your conference*
> *Ask you to speak at their conference*
> *Connect you with a new employee*
> *Offer you a job*

- LinkedIn lets you write notes on each person so use that feature to specify where you met someone along with any personal notes you might want to remember about them.

- Before you accept connections in return, make sure each person is real and relevant to your industry. Check their profile to ensure their employers and job tasks are industry relevant. Make sure they have filled out enough details so you know the person actively uses LinkedIn. Don't link with people whose profiles have almost no details – they're just fishing for your email address.

- Take advantage of LinkedIn groups related to your primary and secondary focus. Find groups by searching for an important keyword, and identify groups that have

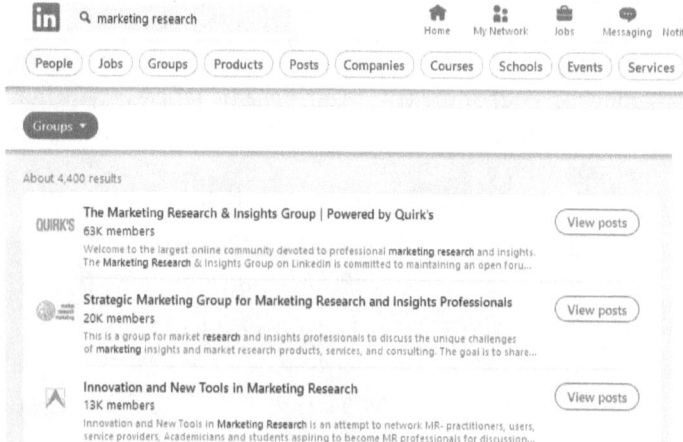

frequent postings, lots of comments, and lots of members. Join 100 groups (or as many as LinkedIn will allow), and then read until your eyeballs fall out from learning so much. The content from these groups will show up in your stream as long as you engage with them.

- Ensure the majority of your posts are business related. Yes, you can talk about your hobbies or your family, but most of your content should specifically address your areas of expertise.

Facebook for friends and family

Many people reserve Facebook for personal friends and family so don't be offended if work colleagues won't friend you or your company page. Each person has the right to decide who they friend, follow, or connect with. If someone doesn't accept your invitation, don't remind them to friend you or ask them why they didn't friend you. They made their decision and it's your turn to respect it.

As with other social networks, Facebook has a groups feature where you can find people who want to share information relevant to your industry. If you want to talk shop on Facebook, groups are the place to go. Just make sure you follow the group rules about what kind of content is allowed. Some will specifically say you cannot share links to your own blog posts. But you can always post your ideas.

Pinterest / Snapchat / Instagram / TikTok / YouTube for visuals

If you are a visual person, consider joining a network that focuses on sharing images or videos. As with other social networks, if you follow the right people and accounts, you'll learn a lot just by reviewing it for 15 minutes a day.

Blogs

Keep a list of every blog that touches your industry perhaps by using an RSS reader like Digg, Feedly, or Flipboard. Start each day by reviewing the list of new posts and choosing a few to read through in more detail.

Webinars

If you love webinars, it's possible to find at least one industry relevant webinar every single day. Even if you can't attend, register for them. You can always watch and learn later. Use the search function on LinkedIn, or whichever professional network you use, to discover the huge range of available webinars.

Local events

Many industry associations have local chapters that host small events on a regular basis. These events are a great way to grow your knowledge base without traveling to a larger conference.

When events are small and have just a few speakers, take good notes and learn as much as you can. When the opportunity arises, personally meet and talk with each expert. In this atmosphere, they are ready and willing to share their knowledge with you. Ask as many questions as you can and be open to every point of view.

How to be a Thought Leader

Coffee

If you're an extrovert, informal chats at a nearby coffee house are perfect. Find out who the local important people in your industry are and see if they'd be interested in chatting with you. Use this time to get to know them personally, not to pump them for free career tips and business advice. Find out how they got into the industry, why they like it, what makes them proud about their work, where they think the future of your industry is going.

A few words of caution. First, asking someone to meet outside the office so you can buy them a coffee is not as great as it sounds. The benefit is yours alone. You are asking them to give up at least 30 minutes for travel time and at least 30 minutes but probably 60 minutes of meeting time in exchange for a $5 coffee. That's 90 minutes they should have spent working on an urgent presentation, making a $10,000 sale, or chilling with their dog. And that's assuming you're the only person who wants to meet them this week.

Second, half of the people you want to meet are introverts. The eight or ten hours they spend in the office working directly with clients and colleagues could very well be more people time than they want. Meeting with you after a full day at work is not in the cards.

In other words, ask to meet for coffee but give people an out. Acknowledge that they might be too busy to meet or that maybe they'd rather answer a couple of questions over email. Since you want them to give you the gift of time, let the choice of how that time is spent be theirs.

3. Write publicly

This tactic will only work if you are a writing machine. And I really hope you are or want to be.

You don't necessarily need to write in all of these places but recognize that everybody has different places across the internet that they like to visit. Start with one tactic and add more over time as you become a better writer.

Start a personal blog

Not all Thought Leaders have a personal blog but I think it is vital. Don't worry if you don't have the technical skill to create a blog because websites like WordPress, Blogger, Medium, LinkedIn, Tumblr and others all provide free platforms where you can sign up and be writing a blog post literally 3 minutes later. If you already use LinkedIn, it requires the least effort and you are guaranteed that people in your industry will be the audience.

Writing a blog gives people a reason to remember you and watch out for you. The most different part is figuring out what to write about. Here are just a couple ideas.

If you meet someone for coffee, ask for permission to write a short post about your meeting. Write about what you learned, what surprised you, and what inspired you. They'll appreciate a bit of positive publicity as a thank you for giving you time. There's no reason why the meeting can't be great for both of you.

If you go to a local chapter event, take good notes and write a post that summarizes what you learned, what you weren't expecting to hear, and why you're intrigued by the topic.

Share what you learned with people who couldn't afford or whose schedules wouldn't enable them to attend.

Once people start to find and read your blog, you might start to see comments from readers. It's polite to write a personal reply to each person who leaves a substantive comment on your blog. It doesn't need to be a long reply but it does need to let them know that you actually read and appreciated their comment.

Thanks for sharing your thoughts. I really like how you differentiated the two key points into subjective and objective features.

Thank you for sharing your story of how you overcame adversity and demonstrated your resilience and capacity to learn. This story will really help other people going through the same issues.

Thank you for leaving a comment. You made my day!

Starting a blog doesn't have to be hard.

- *Blog posts should be as long and as short as necessary. If you make your point well in 150 words, then that's the perfect length. And, if you like to support your opinions with multiple third-party references and end up with a 900 word post, that too is the perfect length.*

- *Given that you're just starting out, aim for 1 or 2 posts each month. Later, when you get into a routine, aim for 1 or 2 posts each week.*

- *Simplify the process by thinking of posts as mini essays. An introduction, 2 or 3 key points, a conclusion. If you know your two points, you're nearly done writing!*

- *Blog posts have more leeway than articles and white papers. Take a bolder, funnier, more personal stance than you might otherwise.*
- *Include links in your post to other experts who wish to offer additional insight.*

Contribute to third party blogs

Next up are local, national, and global association blogs. On top of that, there are even more non-industry blogs. For instance, if you're a market researcher, look for marketing, branding, and journalism blogs. If you're a teacher, look for communications and management blogs. Don't limit yourself by only writing for blogs that focus exactly on your industry. The applicability of your expertise is broader than you realize.

Most importantly, don't wait to be asked to write a post or article. Find publications you admire and look on their website for the submission process. If you can't find a submission process, find out who the editor is and request that information from them. If you've got a writer inside of you, aim to seek out a publication and share a post with them every 4 to 6 months.

Third-party blogs will each have their own unique requirements in addition to wanting to avoid sales pitches. For example, they may require a specific length (e.g., 600 to 1500 words), and they may ask you to include a specific issue in your post. But, as with your own personal blog, you'll likely be welcome to include plenty of links to other authors' posts especially if those links are within the same blog.

Leave comments on blogs

While you're reading blog posts in order to become more knowledge about your industry, notice the opinions you're forming. Do you agree? Disagree? Have an intriguing example or unique experience? Don't wait for the author to ask for your opinions. If you see a comment box, put fingers to keyboard and leave a substantive comment.

The original blogger may be an expert who knows far more than you but your opinion, regardless of your experience, will encourage other people to think critically and further open the dialogue.

There are two important considerations when leaving comments. First, make sure your comment is substantive – offer a new example or a differing opinion. Don't leave a comment at all if it's going to look like one of these:

- *I agree*
- *Exactly*
- *Indeed*
- *What a stupid idea*
- *That's ridiculous*

Substantive comments offer specific ideas about why a post was fantastic, interesting, helpful, or weak. They add value and insight, not confusion and character counts. As with personal blog posts, comments can be really long or really short, but on the shorter side, substantive comments look something like these:

What a great take on management styles. Managers need to appreciate their employees for their ethics and values rather than just getting the job done.

It sounds like you had an amazing time at the conference and learned so much! I'm really glad you feel better informed about the use of artificial intelligence in our industry.

Second, if you're the expert in the field, it's extremely impolite, even rude, to leave a comment such as "I've written about this topic extensively on my blog. Here is the link." Either leave a substantive and relevant comment right there, or don't comment at all. Thought Leaders aren't arrogant and lazy.

Write books

If you like to read and you love to write, I guarantee there is a book in you. Books are a great way to demonstrate your expertise, and they can lead to speaking engagements, requests for assistance, and so much more. Conference organizers are regularly in search of expert authors who've figured out their viewpoints so take full advantage of this.

Just like this book, you don't need to write an 80 000 word tome. This book has about 15 000 words, and it's not too short. Plus, it didn't take 3 years to write. It did take five years of thinking, organizing, testing, and researching, but it took about two months to put fingers to keyboard and write 70 pages of purposeful content.

Find your book.

Tips for writing

Use your real voice.

Don't try to write like Emily Dickenson, Steven King, or the author of your favourite Advanced Statistics textbook. Write like YOU. The only writing style that will get the creative juices flowing coherently is YOUR writing style. If you think ahead to when you're a Thought Leader, people will want to hear and read your voice, not your thoughts in the terrifying voice of Steven King.

DO write whenever you have a free minute.

If you take public transit to work, you have been gifted with two writing opportunities every single day. This might be sufficient to write a blog post. If you are stuck in line, you can write. If you are waiting for a friend to arrive for lunch, you can write. Your mobile device (or a pad of paper and pen) is always ready to receive your words.

Take notes.

Throughout the day, you'll come across ideas that frustrate, annoy, inspire, and excite you. Take notes of those ideas immediately or you will forget them. Later on, when you have time, turn them into real posts.

Let the words flow out of your brain regardless of their quality.

Let the tpyos happen, use bad and inappropriate analogies, and mix up the grammar and spelling. Those things can be fixed, removed, and tidied up later. Get the words out of your brain before you forget the most important points. Edit out the incomprehensible, stupid, and boring parts after you have finished creating insightful content.

Use your writing to figure out what your opinion is.

No one can type as fast as they think which means writing forces you to slow down and ponder what you're saying. Take that opportunity to clarify and expand on your opinions. Think of good examples, alternative interpretations, and opposing viewpoints. Then, punch up your ideas into strong and forceful opinions that will make people think, or, even better, debate and disagree with you.

Your writing will improve over time.

I guarantee it. Turn on the automatic grammar feature of your word processing system, and pay attention to the words and phrases it highlights. You don't have to obey the software but notice the grammar issues it points out and learn from them. Thought Leaders are better able to rise from the pack because they communicate their ideas clearly.

DO aim for good enough.

I'm not 100% happy with anything I've ever written but that doesn't mean my points weren't well-made and well-written. If you aim for perfection, that first comment, blog post, or book will never happen. When you hit 90% satisfaction, click the submit button. Thought Leaders don't ponder a good/great/perfect/excellent/descriptive adjective for half an hour. They publish.

4. Speak virtually

Run your own webinars

Webinars make it easy for anyone to speak and present to a live audience. Even better, it doesn't matter if you're in Sydney and your audience is in Paris, Cairo, and Edmonton. In a global webinar, you can share your expertise, lead question and answer sessions, and engage in personal exchanges with people around the world.

Investing in your own webinar software is an option if you have the funds. But it's not necessary. Many social media channels offer live-streaming capabilities for free, and some company engagement tools (eg., Zoom, Teams) include webinar options as a standard feature.

The only thing you really need to do is attract an audience with some effective marketing. Beyond your own opt-in email list of people who wish to receive webinar invites from you, LinkedIn will probably be your best source to advertise your event.

Participate in guest webinars

If you don't want to be responsible for hosting or managing your own webinar, ask other companies to host you as a guest. Many companies are eager to present guest speakers with a fresh perspective to their audience. Plus, it's easier for them to host webinars with guest speakers who come with a topic rather than develop new content every couple of months.

Search for companies in your industry that regularly host webinars and determine which ones would be a good fit for you. Then employ the tried and true technique – ask them if they'd like a guest webinar speaker.

Once you've been granted a guest spot, be sensitive about your content. Make sure it contains no overt nor covert sales pitches, and make sure it is positioned to be relevant to your host's audience. Besides, as a Thought Leader, the only thing you're selling is your reputation as a trusted expert.

Present at virtual conferences

Virtual multi-day conferences have become quite popular since attendees with even the smallest or no budget can attend. And as a speaker, you won't have to stress about travel arrangements. Freelancers will appreciate not having to pick up the costs for those travel arrangements.

While attendees don't benefit from the in-person experience of traditional conferences, they can enjoy learning in pajamas, with barking dogs and children playing in the background. Most virtual conferences also have backrooms and networking sessions where participants can connect with speakers in a more intimate environment to chat about the conference and industry knowledge.

To get started, search online "Virtual festival" or "Online conference." Virtual conferences often have less strict criteria for accepting speakers so this can be a great opportunity to connect with a large, global audience.

Participate in a podcast

From creating simple YouTube and Vimeo videos, or livecasting on LinkedIn or Facebook, there are plenty of options for people who love to talk.

If you're up to the task, create your own podcast. Since it's your podcast, you can choose whether you'll create 5 minute or 45 minute sessions to suit your needs. But at a minimum, commit yourself to create at least one session per month. This is how you'll grow an audience that looks forward to hearing from you.

Alternatively, if you can't commit to your own monthly podcast, search online for existing podcasts on which you could be a guest. Most podcasters would be delighted if someone asked to be guest and share a fresh point of view on their podcast. Aim to participant in 1 or 2 podcasts each year.

5. Speak in person

For those who like in-person methods of engaging with people, or those who are less keen to use social media techniques, traditional in-person conferences and events are perfect.

Search online for opportunities in your industry using terms like:

- *Call for speakers*
- *Call for papers*
- *Call for workshops*
- *Request for proposals*
- *Request for submissions*
- *Request for speakers*

Consider both small and large, as well as local and international conferences that are broadly relevant in your industry as well as those that serve specialized audience. Don't forget peripheral conferences that seem to be outside of your focus area. Find conference themes you can relate to, review their speaker submission requirements, and submit. Here's the key point, again - Don't wait to be asked!

If you've not spoken at a conference before, focus on opportunities designed for new speakers, for example, shorter sessions (e.g., 15 to 30 minutes) or smaller rooms (e.g., 25 to 75 people). Every speaking opportunity, even those with less exposure, is a good opportunity.

Once you have been accepted as a conference speaker, think carefully about what you can and can't say. The role of a Thought Leader is to share content freely and transparently. If you can't say something, perhaps because it is proprietary or the idea belongs to someone else, then don't bring it up. Telling the audience you can't talk about something is cruel and unusual punishment, like dangling candy in front of me and then running away before I can steal it. Thought Leaders don't hint about or hide content. They share insightful content.

Further, part of sharing insightful content includes being willing to share your presentation materials, whether PowerPoint or white papers. If you don't have your own website, use a site like LinkedIn to upload your content either in time for the conference or immediately after. A bonus is that your content will now be freely available to anyone seeking Thought Leadership, not just the people in your audience.

One of the great things about speaking at a conference is that after you finish speaking and basking in the applause, people will actually want to talk to you. Some will simply say thank you, while others will want to join your for lunch or dunner discussions to learn how they can implement your recommendations.

If all goes well, over time, people will seek you out to speak at future conferences, and submitting to events will become a thing of the past. Until then, aim to speak at 1 or 2 virtual or in-person events each year.

6. Meet people

Attend industry events and conferences

If you aren't ready to speak at events, you can absolutely attend them! The nice thing about conferences is that it is professional and courteous to strike up a conversation with anyone else attending. They are your colleagues and your peers.

Most conference vendors are eager to talk to any and every attendee. This is your opportunity! Make a point of chatting with as many vendors as you can not only to learn more about their business and their offerings, but also to get to know the representative personally. Even if you're not looking to buy anything, both of you will have made a great connection that might benefit another colleague later on.

Deliberately sit beside solo people when choosing your seat at a session. Ask them which sessions they've enjoyed so far and why they chose to attend this session. Ask if they've noticed any general themes across all of the sessions. Most important of all, listen to learn, not to respond.

Find someone sitting by themselves at lunch and join them. Maybe they're waiting for their colleagues or maybe they're too shy or nervous to sit with someone. Either way, you'll meet seven colleagues from the same company, or you'll help someone make a new friend.

Go to group dinners. Suppliers and vendors often invite ten to twenty people to group dinners during events and conferences. If you're a lucky recipient of one of those invitations, go! Yes, the main goal is for the supplier to build personal connections that will hopefully lead to sales. But you too can build personal connections and enjoy a lovely dinner.

Participate in the social events. Most conferences include side activities for participants, perhaps visiting local museums, breweries, or popular attractions. This is a fantastic way to build relationships on a more personal level, particularly since you'll meet people who share some of your interests.

Get personal at local events

Many industry associations have local chapters that host small events on a regular basis. Even if you aren't a speaker, take advantage of the informal event to personally meet and talk with each expert. With smaller events, you'll have far more opportunity to ask questions, generate dialogue, and have meaningful interactions. Even better, stay in touch with them after the event to create longer-term relationships and friendships.

Find group meetups at any time

Go online and search for a meetup group in your industry. Literally search for 'meetup.' These groups will connect you with six or more other people in your local area who want to chat about the same topic. Listen, learn, and create local connections.

Meet individuals one-to-one

If you like chatting with people, informal meetings at a local coffee house are perfect. Find some local experts in your industry are and ask them if they'd be interested in chatting with you. But as we said before, use this time to get to know them personally, not to pump them for free career tips and business advice.

7. Give back to your industry

If you have a favourite association, volunteer with them. Most associations are desperate for help and they'll welcome you with open arms. You could offer to:

- *Organize a chapter event*
- *Prepare marketing materials*
- *Develop a social calendar*
- *Help with their social media accounts*
- *Chair a special project*
- *Offer to draft or comment on a a new paper or guideline*
- *Offer to run training workshops*
- *Find authors for their blog or speakers for their podcast*
- *Nominate yourself to be a board member*

If you have a favourite conference, get in touch with the organization running it and ask how you can contribute. You could:

- *Join the organization committee*
- *Find the keynote speaker*
- *Help source session speakers*
- *Seek out venues*
- *Seek out paid sponsors*
- *Seek out special activities for attendees*
- *Review submissions*
- *Be an on-site guide or runner*
- *Volunteer to be a moderator*
- *Volunteer to moderate table talks*
- *Staff the registration table*

If you have specialized skills in a developing area of your industry, find out if there is an ISO (International Standards Organization) committee in your industry that needs content experts.

Start a group of your own. Are you particularly keen to get women, young people, or marginalized people more involved in your industry? Are you keen to improve perceptions of your field among the general public? Find a few other people willing to push towards that goal and make a concrete plan to change things.

Don't wait to be asked. Do.

8. Mentor colleagues

It keeps coming back to this, doesn't it. If you think about what being a Thought Leader is, it's all about mentoring, teaching, sharing, helping, guiding.

Choosing to become a mentor cannot be taken lightly. Unlike most of the tactics already discussed that are aimed at groups of people, this tactic is aimed at individual people. The lives of individual people will be directly impacted by what you say and do. You need to truly respect and understand the individual, get to know them personally, and try to help them meet their unique goals in life. It won't work and it could even be harmful if this tactic is treated as an item that must be ticked off a list.

You can be wonderful mentor whether you are extraverted, introverted, or scared beyond belief to be seen in the presence of other people. Don't let your personality or preferred method of interaction sway your choice. If you have valuable advice to share, you can find a method of mentoring someone.

Who can you mentor?

Really, anyone. But you have limited time so you need to focus on people who truly need *your* help. Figure out what type of help you are best able to offer, and then identify the type of person who would benefit from that help.

Consider people who are too introverted or shy to ask for help. They may desperately want help but simply can't make the call or send the email asking for help. Being a mentor or Thought Leader means speaking up for people who can't. It's kind of your job.

Consider people who are having a difficult time in their career. Maybe they've been unemployed or have been unable to reach a desired personal or career goal for a long time. If you've achieved that goal, you're in a perfect position to help them evaluate what they've done so far and how they can improve their chances of achieving as well.

Consider people in under-represented groups. For instance, women are under-represented in technical careers. Men are under-represented in primary education careers. Minorities are under-represented in politics. If you are one of the under-represented groups, make it your personal mission to change things. You are proof that people in under-represented groups can do it. And if you're not in an under-represented group, mentoring is proof that people care about helping under-represented groups.

Consider people who have huge potential but don't see it in themselves. That person who always brings up interesting suggestions and unusual insights during team meetings but never gets the chance to act on them. You could help them blossom.

Once you've realized the type of person you'd like to mentor, don't assume they will want you to mentor them. Start simple and non-intrusive. Over time, if they appreciate your efforts, they will ask you for what they want and need.

How can you mentor?

It doesn't matter how you do it. It just matters that you do it.

- *Meet in person. At a café, local chapter meeting, speakers club, or conference.*
- *Talk on the phone*

- *Communicate visually over Skype, Teams, or Zoom*
- *Communicate in writing by email or messaging*
- *Communicate on social by Facebook or LinkedIn*

What can you do?

1. Offer education advice

    a. *Help them choose webinars, workshops, courses, and classes that will push them towards their goals. (e.g., "You should check out that course, it looks perfect for you!)*

    b. *Guide them on their quest towards the right certification for them*

    c. *Encourage them to get certified and help them along the way*

2. Offer career advice

    a. *Match them up with experts in their field so they can learn more about potential career paths (e.g., "You seem to love doing this task. If you want, I can ask Jane to share some tricks she's learned over the years.")*

    b. *Offer resume and cover letter advice*

    c. *Help them understand the types of jobs that could be available to them*

    d. *Help them see the various career paths in their field*

3. Support them at work

    a. *Recommend them for projects, committees, raises, and promotions (e.g., "By the way, I just told your manager that you did a fantastic job on this project.)*

    b. *Encourage them to run training sessions for their colleagues*

    c. *Have them be a second author on a blog post or paper you're writing*

d. *Help them start their own blog*

e. *Nominate them for individual and team awards at work and with industry associations*

4. Offer speaking advice

a. *Encourage them to speak at conferences (e.g., "You were so well spoken in today's meeting. I'd love to help you submit a speaking topic for the fall conference.)*

b. *Help them fill out conference speaking submissions*

c. *Offer to review their speaking materials*

d. *Have them be a co-speaker for a talk you will be doing*

e. *Help them practice their talk and offer advice if they want it*

5. Offer personal advice

a. *Help them identify their strengths and weaknesses (e.g., "I'm so impressed with how you manage so many diverse projects and never lose sight of your priorities."*

b. *Encourage them in tasks that promote their strengths*

6. Be a cheerleader

a. *Congratulate their successes privately and, whenever it's appropriate, publicly*

7. Listen. Just plain listen.

9. Create knowledge

Thought Leaders don't simply reiterate what everyone else is saying. They have new and innovative ideas that challenge how people think. But how do they find enough topics to blather on about? What more is there to say after you've published three blog posts or presented three conference talks? How can there possibly be so much to talk about?

Fortunately, this problem is easy to solve. As you will soon see, everything and everyone around you is inspiration. Keep a notebook handy, whether paper or digital, because once you understand the process, you'll need a lot of space to keep track of your ideas.

Published cartoons, comics, and jokes

If I had any drawing talent, I'd drop a hilarious comic right here. The next best thing I can do is invite you to search for the words comic or cartoon along with your primary or secondary focus. Search for 'education cartoon' or 'journalism comic' or 'construction jokes.' The resulting treasure trove of hilarious and unfunny results is your inspiration.

Don't even bother looking for the best or worst comic. Start with the first one. Why did you laugh or groan or stare blankly at it? Exactly what was funny or stupid or nonsensical? Have you experienced that situation before and how would you or how did you resolve it? Why can't the situation be resolved? Why do some people fail to comprehend the importance of the issue or fail to resolve it no matter how hard they try? What do people need to learn to avoid the problem? Those, my friend, are blog-worthy, conference-worthy, podcast-worthy topics.

Social media

As long as you follow the right people, social media is a never-ending stream of rants, raves, comments, tangents, white papers, webinars, and conversations about your industry. Some content will be directly related to your area of expertise, but others less, much less, so. Regardless of how relevant each piece of content seems, regard each one as inspiration.

As you read, notice whether you smile or smirk or nod your head or pause in puzzlement. Why did you agree or disagree with it? In what ways is your opinion different? Why is a particular message wrong or uninformed? How would you restate it so that people new to the industry would understand it better? Could you use a dataset you own to support or dispute it? All of these are topics. Write them down.

When an irrelevant message crosses your stream, try replacing the irrelevant part with your major content area. Then, continue with the original plan of debating, fixing and creating a fresh post out of the revised message. Thus, *"these are the best chocolate chip cookies I've ever made"* becomes a brand new relevant topic to inspire you:

This is the best political questionnaire I've ever written

This is the best class I've ever taught

This is the best garden I've ever landscaped

Blogs posts and articles

Part of being a Thought Leader means you read a lot of blog posts and articles, and you write substantive comments when the mood strikes. But once you've finished writing a comment, think more thoroughly about what you wrote.

Could you expand on your comment as a separate blog with more details and examples from your personal experiences?

Consider the other comments to that blog post.

Why do you agree or disagree with the other comments?

How would you try to change the mind of those commenters?

Do any of the comments warrant a blog post sized response?

And of course, there is the original blog post itself.

Could you write about the same topic from a different perspective?

Is your opinion the complete opposite and worthy of further explanation?

Could you treat the original post as a 'pro' or 'con' and write the 'con' or 'pro'?

Speakers

Conferences and webinars are fabulous places to discover topics. As you listen to and learn from speakers, notice when you agree or disagree with the points they make, or when you wonder about their methodology or processes.

What unusual or unique experiences have you had that would illustrate their point well?

What questions are audience members raising that you are in a unique position to answer?

What do you completely disagree with?

The point here is not to raise your hand and attempt to publicly one-up the speaker or convince the audience that you are smarter. The speaker probably knows as much or more than you and they're trying to stick to a timeline and stay within the limits of what they're allowed to talk about. The point is for you to generate unique, informed opinions that you can later expand on in your own writing or speaking.

Even better, if you get the chance, chat with the speaker afterwards and see if they'd be interested in writing or speaking about the topic together. When it comes to hashing out ideas and theories, two heads are often better than one.

Non-industry publications

If you are part of an industry that is so small or generic or ignored that there seems to be little inspiration, have no fears. You are covered too. Even the most boring, irrelevant, and trashy daily headlines, celebrity buzz, technology highlights, food blogs, and fashion articles are inspiration.

An article titled "Ten ways to grow ten inches taller and you won't believe the third one" is a perfect topic generator. The media abounds with this sort of ridiculousness and you can use it to your advantage. First, take note that the *style* of this title generates clicks, i.e., reader interest. By copying the title style, you won't need to waste time trying to think of your own cool titles.

As for what you actually write about, certainly you're not going to talk about how to grow ten inches taller. Instead, consider the generic layout of this title:

> *"Ten ways to _____ and you won't believe the third one."*

How many industry relevant business issues can you discuss in this way? A plethora of speaking ideas jumps to mind:

Ten ways to find new sample sources
Ten ways to write a better article
Ten ways to find new construction clients
Ten ways to improve project management
Ten ways to catch logic errors in your writing
Ten ways to display the same piece of data
Ten ways to increase your productivity
Ten ways to find ten more minutes in your day
Ten ways to make meetings shorter
Ten ways to get your boss to listen to you

Here's another popular style of title:

How to get guys to notice you.

Again, replace the irrelevant category with your industry and you're left with myriad writing ideas.

How to get clients to notice you
How to get clients to keep coming back to you
How to get research respondents to pay attention to you
How to get your boss to understand the work you do
How to get investors to fund you
How to get clients to realize the value of your work
How to get the C-suite to fund your pet project
How to get colleagues trained more efficiently
How to get colleagues to work with you

Once you settle on a topic, don't stop there. There is no such thing as one topic. See if you can turn a single post into a series of posts on the same topic. For example, this one post, *"Ten ways to create a better sample,"* could easily become five posts.

Ten ways to create a better quota sample
Ten ways to create a better random sample
Ten ways to create a better stratified sample

Ten ways to create a better snowball sample
Ten ways to create a better convenience sample

Leverage AI

No, it's not cheating. Tools like ChatGPT are a fantastic source for generating ideas. Ask the system for:

10 blog post titles about innovative ways to conduct research

10 reasons to learn about journalism

10 strange ways to teach new ideas to people

10 unexpected uses for a old computer

Not only will you get excellent ideas for the titles themselves, those titles will inspire some great content ideas. Some of the recommended ideas will be old, boring, or ridiculous, but each one idea is a source of inspiration that can lead to an even better idea.

10. Share knowledge

As a Thought Leader, your goal is to guide, mentor, educate, and generally help other people. That includes sharing knowledge generated by other people – even your competitors.

Doing this well can take a lot of time so you'll want to create an achievable plan. We've already decided to aim to speak at one or two events each year, a few podcasts each year, a few blog posts every month, and a few comments every week.

Now, it's time to figure out an everyday plan for sharing content. Lots of ideas follow and it is literally impossible to do all of them. Instead, decide on a tactic and tool that works best for you and be consistent. Every day, find 15 minutes to share your own personal content, and 15 minutes to share content from other people.

Share your own content

You love your social media streams because they are full of interesting and insightful information generated by other people. Now, it's time to add your professional and insightful content to their streams. For example:

- *Links and invitations to all your speaking events, e.g., conferences, podcasts*
- *Links to any blog posts you've written on other websites, e.g., your own website, association websites*
- *Insightful observations about your industry, e.g., innovations, new technologies, new theories*
- *Trends you're seeing arise from all the posts in your stream or the conferences/workshops you've listened to*

- *What you learned from a new project or client you're working with*
- *Reactions to everyday events in terms of how they impact your industry, e.g., how new legislation will affect your processes*
- *Shout-outs with specific details about people and companies in your industry doing a fantastic job*

Share content from other people

At the same time, remember that many other people have interesting and insightful content worth sharing too. You'll want to develop your own set of rules about what is shareworthy so that your own reputation isn't tarnished but consider starting here. Anything you share must:

- *Come from reputable sources*
- *Have a minimum amount of educational, informative, or relevant humorous content, whether text, audio, or video*
- *Not be void of content because you ran out of time but felt you had to share something, anything*
- *Not be an outright sales pitch*
- *Not be misleading, bait and switch*
- *Not force readers through multiple levels of pop-up boxes or similar annoyances*
- *Not be password protected unless they come from industry associations*

It is perfectly acceptable to share articles or content that you disagree with. People need to learn about all valid sides of key issues and be given the opportunity to judge for themselves. Plus, it makes for a great educational conversation when people question your reasons for sharing articles that seem to go against your beliefs.

However, make sure you don't get share content that is unethical, degrading, or harmful for the sake of sharing 'both sides.' There is a difference between sharing valid viewpoints and sharing misinformation or falsely equivalent information.

Finding things to share

No one has the time to search through hundreds of blogs and websites to find inspirational knowledge worth sharing every single day. Fortunately, there are lots of great free tools out there to help you (e.g., Flipboard, AllTop, Pocket, Curator). Others aren't free but it could be worthwhile to test out their free offers in case there's one you would pay for.

LinkedIn: Many people use LinkedIn solely for work related content so you'll have tons of luck finding relevant content here. It's common for some people to write long-form content as status updates, whereas others like to use the dedicated blogging platform.

Find at least one meaningful post or article you love and click on the share button. Add your own substantive comment describing what interested you most about the post, and let your network share in the learning too. Leverage your LinkedIn groups for even more opportunities to learn and share. https://www.linkedin.com/

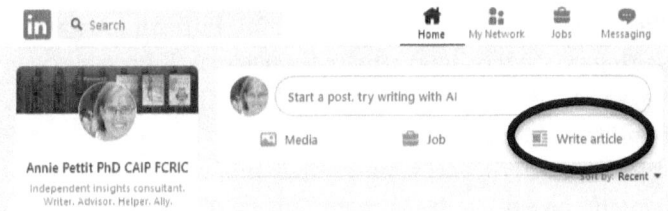

Facebook: Most people use Facebook to share personal content so focus on moderated groups that are specifically related to your general and expert focus areas. The process is the same. Review the recent posts and find one that you love. Then, share the post with a helpful comment. https://www.facebook.com/

Feedly: Also free, Feedly is a fantastic tool for collecting together a lot of RSS feeds from your favourite blogs. It may take some time initially to find those feeds but you'll realize the time savings soon enough. When you've done a good job, you'll end up with a regular stream of highly relevant posts waiting for you every morning. Open your browser, quickly review the titles to find an intriguing insight. Read the post and if it's shareworthy, make the author happy! https://feedly.com

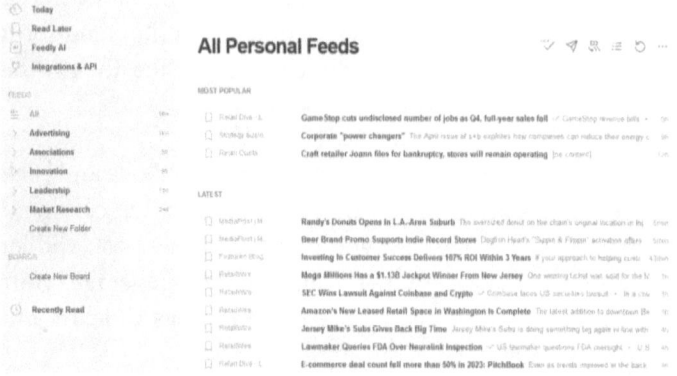

Buzzsumo: Available with a free trial, Buzzsumo is also an aggregator that collects articles from across the internet using keywords that you specify. Just like a traditional internet search, you specify the topic, the date of the content, and the type of content you're interested in. It then rank orders content based on how many times it's been shared on Facebook, LinkedIn, Twitter, and more. It doesn't matter who you follow on the social networks, or if you even use the social networks, you'll get a list of the most popular content related to your desired topic. Find one or two that interest you and then share them with a few details about what caught your attention. https://app.buzzsumo.com/

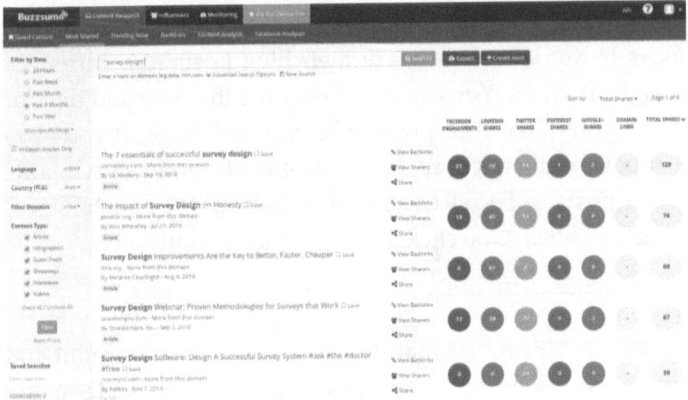

How to share

If you only use one social media website like LinkedIn, it's easy to share your content. Write your notes in the box, add the hyperlink to the original post, and click submit.

However, if your goal is to become a Thought Leader, you probably shouldn't focus all your outbound efforts on just one website. Everyone has their own favourite places to hang out in the digital world and you should consider being present in a couple of places. It doesn't necessarily matter which ones as long as they bring you joy and your target audience likes them too.

To expedite your processes and save time, you're best to find a social media tool specifically designed to help share content in numerous places, often over a scheduled period of time (e.g., Sprout Social, Later, Crowdfire). If you choose this technique, you might spend a couple hours on one day finding and scheduling all your interesting content, and then enjoy watching as the tool releases your work throughout the week.

WordPress: List most blogging tools, WordPress allows users to automatically share their blog posts to a variety of social networks. You can even schedule the time and day for when you'd like your posts to be released. Thus, if you have a super productive day and write 4 posts, you can schedule those posts to be released over 4 days, 8 days, or however long you wish. One click, multiple shares, multiple.

https://wordpress.com/

DLVR.IT: This tool is mainly effective as a paid account and offers two key advantages. First, you can write many different pieces of content and then schedule them to be released on specific days and times. Second, you can connect it to your favourite RSS feeds and schedule that content to be released as well. For example, if you want to support your national association, you could have dlvr.it automatically

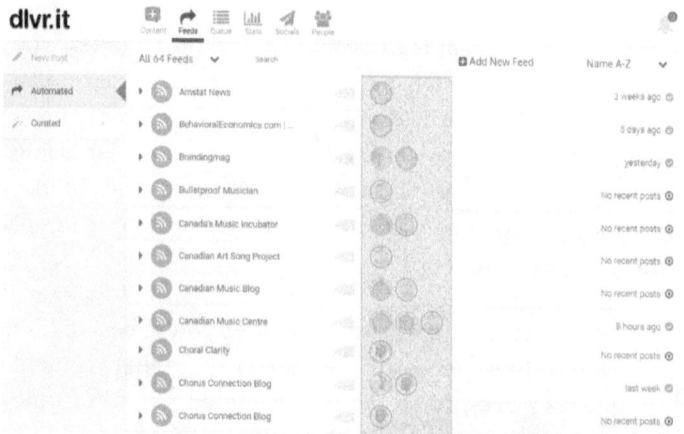

gather and share that association's blog posts on your account. This will help them get even more eyeballs on their important content.

Buffer: Buffer is a great little tool that makes it easy to share content you may find as you work throughout the day. With the browser extension and with one click, it will simplify sharing a post you are currently enjoying across multiple networks simultaneously. You can also manually post items with specified dates and times using their website. I've even used Buffer to time my posts to be released while I speak on stage. Magic!

https://buffer.com/app

How to be a Thought Leader

Thank you
I hope you found this book helpful!
If that was the case, please show your
appreciation for independent authors and
take a couple minutes to

Give it a rating on Amazon!
https://shorturl.at/eip46

How to be a Thought Leader

About the Author

Annie Pettit, PhD, is a Certified Analytics and Insights Professional (CAIP) and Fellow of the Canadian Research Insights Council, the Canadian body for market research. She received a PhD in experimental psychology after completing her dissertation on the data quality of offline and online surveys. Annie has more than twenty years of experience as a professional marketing researcher. She has been an invited speaker at conferences around the world, and has also mentored hundreds of new speakers. In addition to being named an Insights250 Legend, she has won a Ginny Valentine Award, an ESOMAR Excellence Award for Best Paper, an ESOMAR award for Best Methodological Paper, and a David K. Hardin Award.

Connect with Annie on LinkedIn:
https: //www.linkedin.com/in/anniepettit/

Other titles by Annie Pettit available on Amazon
https://shorturl.at/gknHR

Presenters aren't Robots: A practical guide to becoming a fearless and engaging public speaker

People Aren't Robots: A practical guide to the psychology and technique of questionnaire design

7 Strategies and 10 Tactics to Become a Thought Leader

The Listen Lady: A novel and social media research guide baked into one

Technical Books by the Author

Technical books include a practical guide for designing questionnaires, speaking at conferences, techniques for becoming a Thought Leader, and a novel about how to conduct social media listening research. All are available on Amazon.

https://www.amazon.com/author/anniepettit

Puzzle Books by the Author

Gifts for everyone! Research Robot puzzle books make great gifts for students, academics, and professionals in any scientific or research industry! Research Wordsearch is now available on Amazon! Watch for more!

https://t.ly/MsHjQ